PROTECTED
PSALM 91

God's Plan of Protection

John Galinetti

Unless otherwise indicated, all Scripture quotations are taken from the New King James Version of the Bible, copyright © 1979, 1980, 1982, Thomas Nelson, Inc., Publishers.
All Scripture quotations marked KJV are taken from the King James Version of the Bible.

Psalm 91: God's Plan of Protection

ISBN: 978-1-64945-906-0
Copyright © 2020 John Galinetti

Bush Publishing & Associates' books are found everywhere books are sold and on Amazon.com.

For further information, please contact:
Bush Publishing & Associates
Tulsa, Oklahoma
www.bushpublishing.com

Printed in the United States of America.

No portion of this book may be used or reproduced by any means: graphic, electronic or mechanical, including photocopying, recording, taping, or by any information storage retrieval system, without the written permission of the publisher, except in the case of brief quotations embodied in critical articles and reviews.

PSALM 91

God's Plan of Protection

Contents:

Introduction...5

Controlling Fear 9

Psalm 91..13

Four Things Not to Fear........................19

God's Umbrella of Protection...................23

Protection for Today 27

Is Coronavirus God's Judgment? 33

You Have Authority...........................39

Now What? 45

INTRODUCTION

As Americans, there is something that concerns all of us, and it is the subject of security. It is very real to you and it certainly is for me. As I write this book, the word of the Lord that burns within my heart is this, although our country and the entire world are under attack by an invisible enemy called COVID -19, the Coronavirus, we have a covenant of protection. It is stunning to me that one virus could have such a horrible effect upon the lives of so many people. This virus, which began with one germ, has literally shut down our country, as well as crippled the world's economic system. People have been quarantined to their homes and businesses shut down, while the economy, once at an all-time high, has come to a screeching halt. At the time of this writing, over 22 million people are out of work with 10 million people having lost their jobs.

Yet in all of this negative news, there is a beacon of light from the Lord. He has spoken to us through His mighty Word, that He has not given to us a spirit of fear, but a spirit of power, love and a sound mind. (2 Tim. 1:7)

God has strategically laid out, in His Word, a protection plan that is outstanding. This plan is, by far, the greatest insurance plan one could ever have. This protection plan is found in Psalm 91. My heart's cry, for you and the

PSALM 91: GOD'S PLAN OF PROTECTION

entire world, is that you would embrace and take ownership of the promises of protection found in Psalm 91 for yourself and your family. This Psalm is loaded with promises and benefits that are astounding. As you determine to draw near to God and to abide in His presence, you will become so aware of His protection that it will blow your mind away.

God is so good and has nothing but good things in store for you. Even when the Old Testament saints were missing it, big time, it was the Lord who gave the remedy and the answer to their problems.

We see it so clearly in 2 Chron. 7:14:

> If My people who are called by My name will humble themselves, and pray and seek My face, and turn from their wicked ways, then I will hear from heaven, and will forgive their sin and heal their land.

Notice that we have to humble ourselves, pray, seek His face and turn from our wicked ways. The word wicked actually means "twisted." We have to turn from our twisted ways.

The phrase, "If my people," indicates that this word was given to His people.

We see promises and conditions throughout God's Word. The condition here is that we should humble ourselves, pray, seek His face, and turn from our twisted ways.

Introduction

When we do, then the promise indicates,

1. He (God) will hear from Heaven.
2. He will forgive our sin.
3. He will heal our land.

Land is symbolic of anything going wrong in our lives.

As Psalm 91 promises, "No plague, no sickness, no virus, and no disease can stand in the presence of the Lord!" As we determine to love and seek the Lord, He has promised to: never leave or forsake us, protect us in all of our ways, and to satisfy us with long life, showing us His salvation.

This is our battle cry.
This is our confession.
This is our banner.

"No evil shall befall you, neither any plague come near your dwelling. For He shall give His angels charge over you to keep you in all your ways, a thousand will fall at your side and ten thousand at your right hand but it will not come near you, in Jesus Name. Amen."

CHAPTER 1
CONTROLLING FEAR

You and I are witnessing and living through something we've never lived through before and that is this pandemic, COVID-19. It has produced an insane amount of fear within people in our country and even around the world.

World history is filled with examples of people walking in fear. In 1918, the avian-borne flu resulted in 50 million deaths worldwide. The first wire service reports of a flu outbreak in Madrid led to the pandemic being called the "Spanish flu." In 1957, the Asian flu became widespread in England where, over six months, 14,000 people died. It was followed by a second wave in 1958, resulting in an estimated 1 million deaths globally, with 116,000 deaths in the United States alone. More recently there have been the HIV and SARS attacks to the immune system. And at the time of the writing of this book, March of 2020, the World Health Organization announced that the COVID-19

PSALM 91: GOD'S PLAN OF PROTECTION

virus was officially a pandemic, after barreling through 114 countries in three months and infecting millions of people. The spread is nowhere even close to being finished.

We know that God has not given us, as believers, a spirit of fear, but rather a spirit of power, love, and a sound mind. (2 Tim. 1:7). Be encouraged in this and know that when you seek the Lord, He will deliver you from all of your fears.

It's a very real fear for millions of Americans that have never experienced this before. They are asking, "Am I safe? Will I lose my job? How long will I survive? Where will my income come from? What will happen if I get ill or sick?" Yet, God says in His Word that He is an ever-present help in the time of trouble. (Ps. 46:1). There is no better time than now to seek the Lord in the times that we're living in. We're living in the end times. These are the last of the last days and it's exciting to see what God is doing. I believe that in the midst of this calamity, in the midst of this pandemic, God is not only moving in an incredible way within the people of Mount Hope Church but around America and around the world. This could be the church's finest hour. We, the church, meaning the body of Christ, have an opportunity to demonstrate our joy and composure, a composure that we have because of the peace of Jesus Christ.

In regards to fear, David wrote Psalm 34 and said,

Chapter 1: Controlling Fear

"I sought the Lord and He heard me and He delivered me from all of my fears." (Ps. 34:4)

The love of God casts out all fear and fear has no place in our life. Even though people around us are experiencing fear, for us, as Christians, fear should have no part in our life.

Jesus did warn us by saying something that most of us wish he had never said, being, "These things I have spoken to you that in me you might have peace. In the world you will have tribulation." (John 16:33) The word "tribulation" is often used in the subject of Bible prophecy but it is used by Jesus to mean trouble or troubling times which are happening right now. He says, "But in me you will have peace. But be of good cheer. I have overcome the world."

The greater one lives within us and gives us joy. We can have the peace of God that passes all understanding in the innermost part of our life. That's what Jesus was talking about. In the inner world and inner kingdom of our life is where revelation has to occur. The Word of God must settle in us in the innermost kingdom of our life. And when that revelation of Christ becomes real in us, we'll have peace, contentment, and great resolve on the outside as well. That's why Jesus said those word in John 16.

As Christians, we are at war with this virus on two fronts. The first front is the natural side. Washing your

PSALM 91: GOD'S PLAN OF PROTECTION

hands, using hand sanitizer, and social distancing are natural things that we can do to try to control the virus. But there is also the spiritual side to the battle. When you combine the natural with the spiritual, it breaks the devil's back and stops this virus, and any other sickness, in its tracks.

Personally, I say the words of Psalm 91 over my life, probably fifteen to twenty times a day. I don't do it for attention but because I don't want to die. I hate sickness. It saddens me when I hear of people in our congregation, family members, and distant friends, who have been affected by this horrid plague. It hurts me and it bothers me. I don't like being sick and I know you don't either.

Matthew 8:17 says, "Himself took our infirmities and bore our sicknesses." The word "bore" is the Greek word, "bastazo" which means to lift, bear, and take away with the idea of total removal. I'm so glad that our Savior died for our sins and sicknesses. Because He did, we can lay hold of those covenant rights and speak God's Word. I encourage you to do the same.

CHAPTER 2
PSALM 91

Psalm 91:1-16

He who dwells in the secret place of the Most High Shall abide under the shadow of the Almighty. I will say of the Lord, "He is my refuge and my fortress; My God, in Him I will trust." Surely He shall deliver you from the snare of the fowler and from the perilous pestilence. He shall cover you with His feathers, and under His wings you shall take refuge; His truth shall be your shield and buckler. You shall not be afraid of the terror by night, nor of the arrow that flies by day, Nor of the pestilence that walks in darkness, nor of the destruction that lays waste at noonday. A thousand may fall at your side, and ten thou-

PSALM 91: GOD'S PLAN OF PROTECTION

sand at your right hand; but it shall not come near you. Only with your eyes shall you look, and see the reward of the wicked.

Because you have made the Lord, who is my refuge, even the Most High, your dwelling place, no evil shall befall you, nor shall any plague come near your dwelling; For He shall give His angels charge over you, to keep you in all your ways. In their hands they shall bear you up, lest you dash your foot against a stone. You shall tread upon the lion and the cobra, the young lion and the serpent you shall trample underfoot.

"Because he has set his love upon Me, therefore I will deliver him; I will set him on high, because he has known My name. He shall call upon Me, and I will answer him; I will be with him in trouble; I will deliver him and honor him. With long life I will satisfy him, And show him My salvation."

In the present time that we live, with the threat of war, pandemics, and other things occurring, it is very important to know that we are protected by God.

Psalm 91 is our greatest promise of protection during these

Chapter 2: Psalm 91

times. The Old Testament was written in Hebrew and I want to bring out some of the meanings of these Hebrew words.

Psalm 91 says this, "He who dwells in the secret place of the Most High shall abide under the shadow of the Almighty." The word "dwell" means to "set up shack." In a practical sense, it means that when you praise God and follow the Lord, you're setting up shack with the Lord. Thirty-five years ago, I met a blonde, blue-eyed girl. To me, it was very evident that she was casting longing eyes upon me. My attraction to her was so evident that I said to her, "Seeing that you love me and I love you, would you dwell with me?" That's what marriage is. And she answered, "Yes, I will dwell with you." We've been setting up shack for thirty-five years now. God created marriage to get better and better as the years go by. Although you might have a difficult year from time to time, God has designed marriage to get better and better, the longer you set up shack with one another.

The word "dwell" also means to stake a claim and set up shop in the secret place.

This is a benefit to the believer who abides in the presence of God. All of the promises in Psalm 91 are all contingent on the first two verses. It says, he or she who dwells in the secret place of the Most High God. God's promises of protection are all contingent upon us abiding

PSALM 91: GOD'S PLAN OF PROTECTION

in His presence.

So, Christian, this is for you. "No evil shall befall you neither any plague come near your dwelling. For he shall give his angels charge over you to protect you in all of your ways." (Ps. 91:10-11) "A thousand shall fall at your side and ten thousand at your right hand but it shall not come near your dwelling." (91:7)

The phrase, "under the shadow" means under the defense system of God. You have a defense system right now. You are protected under it.

The word "Almighty" means "the all sufficient one." He is all sufficient and He is the all sufficient one. He is also known here as El Shaddai, a Hebrew name that God revealed to the children of Israel. Through His revealed names, God was revealing a part of His character to them. He wanted to reveal a side of who He was and He wanted them to claim the benefit of that Hebrew name and allow it to materialize in their lives. He was saying, "I am El Shaddai, the God who is more than enough." Amen! He is more than enough.

When you magnify El Shaddai, He loves it. Imagine God looking from heaven and saying, "Look, someone is worshipping me down there in Grand Blanc, Michigan. Look at them! They're worshipping me. I love it." Now, imagine Jesus coming over and saying, "I'm so glad that

Chapter 2: Psalm 91

they are praising you, Heavenly Father." Someone might ask, "where is the Holy Spirit?" He's whipping around on the earth right now. That's what He is doing. He's out convicting, revealing, working, and opening the eyes of our understanding. Isn't it great? I read the end of the book and we win. It's so good.

As we deal with the issues and struggles of life, it is awesome to know that God is protecting us and that He is the one who can be more than enough. He's El Shaddai, the God who is more than enough. You're under the defense system of the Lord.

Verse two goes on to say, "I will say of the Lord, He is my refuge and my fortress; My God, in Him I will trust." The word "say", in the Hebrew, means to talk the same way that God talks. That's exactly what it means. Many times, we face a problem and we begin to talk the problem. You see, it's not that we are not acknowledging the existence of a problem, but rather, we are acknowledging God and saying who He is. We proclaim that He is our healer. We proclaim that He is our protector. We proclaim that He is saving and intervening in our life. You say it. The Father's message is: say and talk the same way that God does.

Verse three says, "Surely He shall deliver you from the snare of the fowler and from the perilous pestilence." "Surely" means absolutely. The word "snare" speaks of the

PSALM 91: GOD'S PLAN OF PROTECTION

multi-faceted traps of the enemy. Because you're scooting up under the big feathers of the Lord, He's going to give you eyes like an eagle. Eagles flying high above the earth can see the prey down below and also any traps they may encounter.

"Perilous pestilence" refers to the most talked about plague of the day.

What would that be? In 2020, it was the Coronavirus. Analysts are saying that the airlines will lose billions of dollars in airfare if the pandemic hits the way that it is projected to. We can say with surety, "I'm protected from the coronavirus." Why is that? Because we're abiding under the shadow and defense system of the Lord.

During this time, it is amazing the tools that the enemy has used to isolate people. Let's guard against magnifying the virus over the greatness of our God.

CHAPTER 3
FOUR THINGS NOT TO FEAR

Psalm 91:5-6
You shall not be afraid of the terror by night, Nor of the arrow that flies by day, Nor of the pestilence that walks in darkness, Nor of the destruction that lays waste at noonday.

In this passage, notice the four things that God does not want us to fear:

1. Terror by night

In the day and time that we live in, people hear sounds outside their home and imagine, "What is that?" Because of fear, they invest in a security system so that they can monitor everything going on around them. I'm not advising against that; it's none of my business. However, it is a fact that many Americans are obsessed with the issue of security. They are

PSALM 91: GOD'S PLAN OF PROTECTION

freaking out, thinking that they must have the latest and most advanced security system, because of the terror by night. Remember, we have a defense system in God.

2. The arrow that flies by day

In the Hebrew, this refers to anything that is designed to hurt you.

3. The pestilence of terminal disease

This also includes pests that destroy livestock and human life. Even my cat Cooper, who is the size of a dog, is blessed because he lives in my house. Even though at times he annoys me, he's blessed, because he's under a covering of protection. Your animals will be blessed.

4. Destruction at noon day

That means that midlife crisis does not have to take you down. The Bible mentions a man by the name of Caleb. Caleb was eighty years old, but operated like he was forty. He must have dwelt in the secret place of the Most High. He saw things through the lens of the Word of God and not the public opinion of his day. Joshua asked him if he was sure he could take this mountain. His response was, "I'm 80, but I feel like I'm 40, and I'm going to go take that mountain." Others saw Caleb as an oddity, simply because

Chapter 3: Four Things Not to Fear

he was an "on fire" believer for the Lord, living underneath the umbrella of God's protection. I can't wait to meet Caleb when I go home to be with the Lord. I plan to tell him how awesome I think he was for taking the mountain.

Psalm 91:7-10

A thousand may fall at your side, And ten thousand at your right hand; But it shall not come near you. Only with your eyes shall you look, And see the reward of the wicked.

Because you have made the Lord, who is my refuge, Even the Most High, your dwelling place, No evil shall befall you, Nor shall any plague come near your dwelling.

Notice that the plague will not come near your dwelling. Why? Because you're serving the Lord and living for God. You're dwelling in the secret place. He's giving you eagle eyes and the wisdom to understand and to make the right move at the right time.

Verse 11 goes on to say, "For He shall give His angels charge over you, to keep you in all your ways." No matter where you go, God is watching over you to protect

PSALM 91: GOD'S PLAN OF PROTECTION

you. It is important to hear His Spirit, avoid operating in foolishness, and hear what He is saying to you.

We build that refuge and habitation through praise. Praise becomes the dwelling place for God's presence. In other words, the Bible says that God inhabits the praises of His people. Hebrews 13:15 says, "…let us continually offer the sacrifice of praise…the fruit of our lips, giving thanks to His name." Yet, some people still don't get it. The Bible talks so much about blessing the Lord at all times and continually praising God, which is the key. Praising causes the promises of God to become real in our life. Faith is not a magic wand or a force of mystery. It is a reality to those who really press in to the things of God.

Here at Mount Hope Church, we're teaching believers how to live victoriously, grow up spiritually, and motivating them toward the promises of God so that they can live life to the fullest. Our message is that they can have what God says they can have.

I encourage you to read Psalm 91 and personalize the words to yourself so that it becomes real to you. Psalm 91 has been my mantra through this whole pandemic.

CHAPTER 4
GOD'S UMBRELLA OF PROTECTION

Take an umbrella, for instance. In the same way that you stand under an umbrella to keep you from the rain, you are under the umbrella of God's protection. As you serve the Lord and magnify Him, you create an atmosphere of understanding that God is protecting you. That is what is so great about serving God. The world around us doesn't have that understanding and protection. However, when a person accepts Jesus Christ, they come underneath the umbrella of God's salvation. It is in that moment that they receive the gift of eternal life which is free. "For whoever calls on the name of the Lord shall be saved." (Rom. 1:13) When a Christian surrenders to the lordship of Jesus, they come under the umbrella of God's protection and all of His blessings as well.

We are blessed to be a blessing. It's one thing to receive the promise of a promised land and it's an entirely

PSALM 91: GOD'S PLAN OF PROTECTION

different thing to actually go into the promised land, defeat the giants, possess the mountains, and obtain the blessings that God has in store. You're under the umbrella of God's protection. When you and I magnify the Lord, we create an atmosphere and an awareness of that protection in our life.

Throughout history, God has always protected His people from wrath. Always! Let's take for example Noah. Noah and his family are a type and symbol of the body of Christ in the Old Testament. Noah lived to the ripe old age of 950 years. Many people throughout the Old Testament lived similarly very long lives. Can you imagine that? Yet, because of the wickedness of man's heart, God shortened man's life to 120 years. Man's days were shortened because of the evilness in his heart.

In the days of Noah, it was very similar to today. There was a lot of evil in the world. God spoke to Noah saying, "I want you to build me an ark." And so, God gave him the plans for the ark and Noah began to construct it. For a hundred years Noah preached and didn't get one convert. What a bummer man. But Noah kept declaring that it was going to rain. He proclaimed, "The rain is coming. There is a rain coming. God is going to pour out a rain." In that time in history, it had never ever rained before. God had sustained the vegetation of the earth through the dew of the earth. But it had never rained up to that time. Then,

Chapter 4: God's Umbrella of Protection

all of a sudden, the depths broke up, judgment came, and the rains fell. Even though God was trying to warn the people, through the prophet Noah, they wouldn't believe him. Can you just imagine CNN being there? The reporter says, "There's this man with a big beard out here and he's saying it's going to rain. Let me tell you a little bit about this man named Noah. He's a little strange - I'll tell you that. But he's saying it's going to rain, whatever that is." But it rained just as Noah said it would, and during the flood, Noah and his family were protected from destruction in the ark. In the same way, the church will be protected in the hour of God's wrath. We will be evacuated and taken up before the time of Jacob's trouble, the Bible says. Noah released the bird out of the ark and it came back with an olive branch giving Noah indication that the waters were dissipating.

As the waters receded, God spoke to Noah saying, "I'm going to make my covenant with you." A covenant is a binding agreement between two parties that could only be broken by death. It was a very powerful, powerful word. I want you to know that you are in covenant with the living Lord Jesus Christ today. God cut covenant with the world when Jesus shed His blood. Covenant is a coming into agreement. People in the Old Testament would cut their arm, then slap them together, and begin pronouncing prom-

25

PSALM 91: GOD'S PLAN OF PROTECTION

ises over one another. Common examples of the promises made were: a) Everything that is mine is yours. B) When you go to war, I will go to war with you. Confessions were also made. This was the type of covenant that God made with Noah.

The Lord commanded Noah to go into the earth and multiply - the same command that God gave to Adam he gave to Noah. Then God said, "I will put the rainbow in the sky to let you know that I will never flood the earth again." (Gen. 9:13) The token of the covenant was the rainbow. Today, every time it rains you see the rainbow. When I see a rainbow I say, "Thank you Jesus." Every time you see a rainbow, it is God's covenant to Noah's descendants, which includes us. We are protected from the hour of God's wrath, the ark being symbolic of God's protection. Noah is symbolic of the body of Christ in the Old Testament and the rainbow is a physical sign that God will never flood the earth again.

CHAPTER 5
PROTECTION FOR TODAY

Now, prophetically speaking, we're in the same days as Noah was. In Matthew 24:37-39, Jesus spoke these words, "But as the days of Noah were, so also will the coming of the Son of Man be. For as in the days before the flood, they were eating and drinking, marrying and giving in marriage, until the day that Noah entered the ark, and did not know until the flood came and took them all way, so also will the coming of the Son of Man be." I'm so glad that we have discernment in the end times. You and I can see these things and not get discouraged about what we hear in the news. For the world around us, things are going to get worse, but for us, things are going to get better. I read the end of the book and we win!

Paul, speaking about prophecy in 1 Thessalonians 4, refers to the rapture of the church. Just like God protected Noah, He's going to protect you from the hour of his wrath.

PSALM 91: GOD'S PLAN OF PROTECTION

Paul writes,

1 Thessalonians 4:16-18

For the Lord himself will come down from heaven, with a loud command, with the voice of the archangel and with the trumpet call of God, and the dead in Christ will rise first. After that, we who are still alive and are left will be caught up together with them in the clouds to meet the Lord in the air. And so we will be with the Lord forever. Therefore encourage one another with these words.

The phrase "caught up," in the Greek, means to be raptured away. Paul uses the Greek word "harpazo," which carries the meaning to seize, catch away, pluck, or to snatch away with irresistible force. How many of you like vacuuming your home? When you vacuum, those little particles cannot resist the power of your vacuum cleaner. I liken it to that. We're going to be going about our daily routine when we get caught up in a twinkling of an eye, in an atomic second, like Paul said. It is really exciting to know that God would evacuate His people right off the earth right before the great tribulation period. This is proof, once again, that

Chapter 5: Protection for Today

God protects His people from the hour of wrath.

The second example of God's protection is absolutely insane. The children of Israel were in Egypt. They were in slavery and Moses goes to Pharaoh. In that day, the people regarded Pharaoh as God, and Pharaoh conducted himself as if he were God. But he was just a man. As Pharaoh appeared around Egypt, people would bow before him with feathers and various articles of adoration, worshipping Pharaoh. So, Moses has the fiery bush experience with God on the mountain, where God instructs Moses to go and set His people free. God says, "I want my people to worship me." God speaks to Moses saying, "I am that I am. I am El Shaddai, the God who is more than enough. That's all you need to know."

Moses responds to God, "How am I going to talk?" You see, Moses had a stuttering problem, yet he became one of the greatest leaders of all time. God replies to Moses, "I'm going to let Aaron help you out. I'm going to let Aaron do the talking for you." So, they go before Pharaoh and Moses says, "God spoke to me to tell you to let MY people go!" At that time there were over two million Jewish slaves in Egypt. Pharaoh would not do it. His response was, "Ha, get out of here. I don't even want you in my presence." Moses returns to Pharaoh again with Aaron and the message to, "let my people go!" Pharaoh's reply

PSALM 91: GOD'S PLAN OF PROTECTION

is the same, "No, get out of here." A third time Aaron says, "God says, let my people go so that we may worship our God. And if you don't, the Lord spoke to me that he's going to bring calamity on the land of Egypt." Once again, Pharaoh's response is, "Ha, ha, ha. Get out of here!" Just like in the Charlton Heston film, The Ten Commandments, God poured out ten plagues. Long before Hollywood made it into a movie, it actually happened.

Now, what is so incredible about this story is that not one plague touched the land of Goshen, where God's people lived. Goshen was a huge mass of a suburb, more like a city in the land of Egypt. All the plagues were poured out but not one of them touched the Land of Goshen. Why? Because the children of Israel, just like you and me, were in covenant with Almighty God. Amen!

Today, we've got a much better covenant, established upon better promises. We get everything the children of Israel did, plus more! The water became blood, that was the first plague. The second plague was frogs. Imagine it - frogs in their microwaves and frogs in their refrigerators. When they woke up, there were probably frogs under their pillow, in their pillow, and sitting on their face. That's a radical summarization but it was true. Yet, in the Land of Goshen there were not any more frogs than the inhabitants were used to. There were so many frogs in Egypt that they

Chapter 5: Protection for Today

were piled into huge heaps. People who liked to eat frog legs were probably having a feast.

Then there were lice and flies. On the Upper Peninsula of Michigan there are flies that bite. Also, during this time, the livestock in Egypt became super skinny while the livestock in the Land of Goshen stayed strong and healthy. There were boils that broke out on the skin of all of the Egyptians and their cattle while in the Land of Goshen, there was nothing.

There was hail that destroyed the vegetation in Egypt. The Land of Goshen, on the other hand, had no hail. None whatsoever.

Then there were locusts who came and devoured what the hail didn't destroy. There were locusts, millions and millions of them everywhere. But in the Land of Goshen there were no locusts. There was darkness over the face of the earth that had never happened before. While Egypt was in darkness, the Land of Goshen enjoyed light. What a testimony of living in covenant with Almighty God. It was awesome. In the Land of Goshen not one plague materialized. Then the plagues culminated with the death of the first born. What an astounding display of God protecting his people from calamity and disaster.

You and I have a canopy of protection over our lives because we serve God. Be careful what you allow into your

PSALM 91: GOD'S PLAN OF PROTECTION

eye gates and in your ear gates. It's important to always look into the Word of God and speak the Word of God.

There are the prophets of the land and the prophets of the Lord. The prophets of the land will only give you the natural side such as wash your hands and social distancing. They share the natural side of things but never give you the spiritual side - the authority side that we have in Jesus.

The awesome thing about speaking God's Word is that you can be in your house, in your car, simply going around, and pray Psalm 91. As you say it, you believe it, creating an atmosphere of faith in your house and around you.

CHAPTER 6
IS CORONAVIRUS GOD'S JUDGMENT?

People ask, "Is this God judging America?" First of all, where or when, in the four gospels, did we ever see Jesus hurting anybody? Jesus never brought sickness or disease into the planet. Jesus is not hurting people with a virus, the plague, a sickness, disease, calamity or pain and suffering. We will never, ever find that in the four Gospels.

If there is ever a time when people needed a promise, this one verse sets the record straight. It is one verse that addresses God's stance during our current pandemic.

<u>John 10:10</u>
The thief does not come except to steal, and to kill, and to destroy. I have come that they may have life, and that they may have it more abundantly.

33

PSALM 91: GOD'S PLAN OF PROTECTION

We see very clearly and emphatically that it is the devil who has come to steal, kill and destroy.

You can see the two prominent natures in this one verse. Seeing the contrast of these two natures will help you to share with other people. When others wonder if God is the cause of this, or wonder why things are happening as they are, God's Word clears up all confusion. In John 10:10, we see the nature of the devil, which is to kill, steal and destroy. Then we see the nature of God, through Jesus Christ, which is to give life and to give life with abundance.

Satan came to take from you, to steal from you, and to eventually destroy you. Satan hates God. Satan hates Israel. Satan hates Jesus and he hates anybody who identifies with Him. That's why there is so much destruction in the world today.

According to the scriptures, Lucifer was kicked out of heaven and came down to earth with great wrath. Jesus came to give you life and life with abundance. One nature takes and the other gives. It's so simple to see and understand. Satan's nature takes and wants to kill while the nature of Jesus is to give and to give with abundance. Seeing this truth clears up clouded views on the nature and the character of God.

If we want to know what the Heavenly Father is really like, all we have to do is look to His Son, Jesus. What

Chapter 6: Is Coronavirus God's Judgment?

is God's nature like? What is His character like? Most of us have heard the phrase, "like father like son." That's exactly true of Jesus Christ and the Heavenly Father. The Heavenly Father's character, nature, and disposition is demonstrated through the person of Jesus Christ. That's why at the birth of Christ, the scriptures say, "and they shall call His name Immanuel, which is translated, God with us."

I love being a Christian on this planet. We've got so much to look forward to. We have the promises of God. We have the power of God on the inside. We have so much at our disposal with the angels of God protecting us. Because of these truths, let's make sure we're continuing to say, "No evil will befall us and neither any plague come near our dwelling."

When you speak those words, it leaps into operation and it causes faith to come alive. You see, faith can lie dormant in your heart and in your spirit. Faith must be released out of your mouth for it to create an atmosphere for God to move mightily in your life.

One day, you invited Jesus Christ to come into your life. You believed in your heart and you confessed with your mouth, and salvation came into you. It was sealed on the inside of you when you were saved. The same principal operates with the promises of God.

PSALM 91: GOD'S PLAN OF PROTECTION

Hebrews 1:1-3

God, who at various times and in various ways spoke in time past to the fathers by the prophets, has in these last days spoken to us by His Son, whom He has appointed heir of all things, through whom also He made the worlds; who being the brightness of His glory and the express image of His person.

Jesus is the exact cookie cutter image of our Heavenly Father. At Christmas, it is a time for cookies. I happen to like cookies all the time. In our home, we have cookie cutters with the shapes of Christmas trees, wreaths, and even Santa Claus. We take the cookie cutter, which is the exact image of the shape that we want, cut the dough, put it on the cookie sheet, and put it in the oven. Jesus is the exact cookie cutter image of the character and nature of the Father. If you want to know what the Heavenly Father is like, all you have to do is look at the Son.

Now, concerning COVID-19, let me say this. It is amazing to me how one germ and virus can cause such pain and suffering in our land. It has arrested our nation causing a roaring economy to come to a screeching halt. It is amazing what one germ and virus can do. I've been asked by

Chapter 6: Is Coronavirus God's Judgment?

others if I feel this is God judging America? Is this virus God's doing? Let me clear some things up right now. God will not send pain or suffering into someone's life. That is not the Lord at all. It is the devil, not God, who is perpetuating this wicked virus in the earth today.

Some insurance companies are calling COVID-19 an act of God which is contrary to what my Bible says. My Bible states, "how God anointed Jesus Christ of Nazareth with the Holy Spirit and power who went about doing good and healing all that were oppressed of the devil." (Acts 10:38)

This one germ and virus has been released from the pit of hell. Jesus came to bring good not evil. Even in the Old Testament God said, "I will put none of the diseases on you which I have brought on the Egyptians. For I am the Lord who heals you." (Exodus 15:26). He also promises, "….and He will bless your bread and your water. And I will take sickness away from the midst of you." (Exodus 23:25). In the Hebrew it means that God will aim sickness in a different direction. I often say, there's no better way to live on earth than being a Christian. There's nothing like it. It is incredible being a Christian during this time, in this generation right now. It is absolutely exciting.

38

CHAPTER 7
YOU HAVE AUTHORITY

One day as I was picking up a folder from a business office, there was a gentleman exiting the building, who looked at me and said, "Hey, where's your mask?" I turned around and answered, "My mask is Psalm 91 and I have a canopy of protection from the Lord over my life." He asked, "Well, how is that?" I replied, "Psalm 91 says, no evil shall befall you neither any plague come near your dwelling. For he will give his angels charge over you to keep you in all of your ways. A thousand will fall at your side and ten thousand at your right hand but it will not come near you." He responded, "Wow, man, that is awesome. I need to memorize that and get it in my heart and mind." It is true and absolutely something that you should do.

You need to get the Word of God into your heart and into your mind. Memorize it and speak it. When speaking God's Word, it materializes in our life and releases tremen-

PSALM 91: GOD'S PLAN OF PROTECTION

dous power. Proverbs tells us that death and life is in the power of the tongue. (Prov. 18:21) When we speak God's Word over our life and circumstances, it carries such power with it that it decapitates fear from your life.

Luke 10:17-19

Then the seventy returned with joy, saying, "Lord, even the demons are subject to us in Your name."

And He said to them, "I saw Satan fall like lightning from heaven. Behold, I give you the authority to trample on serpents and scorpions, and over all the power of the enemy, and nothing shall by any means hurt you."

Is that the picture of the American believer today? Is that a picture of what is happening right now? We come to church to get understanding, to receive inspiring teaching, and to hear from the Word of God. We learn that we're the ones to be in control, not over people and their wills, but rather over the things that are constantly lying to us. However, in some cases, we're the ones being controlled. Whoever you are, you are to pray that God's kingdom come, and that

Chapter 7: You Have Authority

His will be done. We're to take back what the enemy has stolen from our life, our city, and our region. That's why Satan hates it when people get all fired up for God and start going to church. He's roaming the earth, seeking to devour us, while we are gathered in church. The devil must be beside himself wondering what he's going to do to us next. Our response will always be, "Freak out, devil! We have authority over you and we're going to trample you under our feet."

In terms of controlling fear, be careful who you're listening to. Personally, I can only listen to so much of the news. If you listen too much to the prophets of the land and all the newscasters, you will only hear bad news. The media is doing their job but they tend to dwell on all the bad news. God gives us the good news. The good news is that the greater one lives on the inside of us. We have victory through God, and when we seek Him, God sheds His power and grace upon us even more. It's so awesome to know that.

When Adam and Eve broke God's commands, they committed high treason in the sight of God. Satan entered in and that's where all the death, decay, and sickness came. Because Satan was the originator of sin, sickness and disease, he is considered the god of this age.

In 2 Corinthians 4 Paul writes, "If our gospel is hid and is hid to them that are lost in whom the god of this

41

PSALM 91: GOD'S PLAN OF PROTECTION

world has blinded their eyes to the glorious life of the Gospel of Jesus Christ." (2 Cor. 4:3-4) Also in Ephesians 2, Paul writes, "in which you once walked according to the course of this world, according to the prince of the power of the air, the spirit who now works in the sons of disobedience…." (Eph 2:2)

According to Psalm 24:1, the earth is the Lord's and the fullness thereof but Satan is the god of this age, as a result of the sin of Adam and Eve. People have always asked the question, "If there is such a good God, who loves and cares for everyone, why is there so much pain and suffering in the earth?" It is because the god of this world, the devil, is creating it. He has come to kill, steal and destroy. Jesus is come to give you life and life with abundance. Notice the insight of Ephesians 2:1-2 from the New Living translation: "Once you were dead because of your disobedience and your many sins. You used to live in sin, just like the rest of the world, obeying the devil—the commander of the powers in the unseen world. He is the spirit at work in the hearts of those who refuse to obey God."

The devil is working in the unseen world to kill, steal and destroy, while the nature of God is to give life and life with abundance. Now, in the midst of all this darkness and in the midst of all this chaos, God sends His Son into

Chapter 7: You Have Authority

the world to bring salvation, healing, and deliverance to all who would look to Him.

You have authority and power over all the work of the enemy. That's you and that power is resident in you right now. You and I are carriers of that power and authority right now. We're taking back what the enemy has stolen. We're taking back our healing. We're taking back the soundness of our mind. We're taking back our prosperity. We're taking back all the good things that the devil has stolen from us. The devil comes to kill, steal and destroy. Jesus is come to give life and to give it more abundantly. And with that, Jesus gives joy, peace, goodness, salvation and eternal life.

Sickness and disease, death and decay, evil and wickedness, and Satan's works of darkness all rode into the world on that one disobedient act in the Garden of Eden. That's where it all started. God never created that. The earth is the Lord's and the fullness thereof, but the earth is under the influence of Satan. Satan has a lease on this planet and he knows that his time is short. He is doing his best to rock this world and to manipulate people to sin. It is when people get involved in sin that Satan gains access into their life. But you and I, as born-again Christians, have authority over him. Satan is under our feet. When Jesus rose from the dead, He defeated death, hell, and the grave and He's alive forevermore.

PSALM 91: GOD'S PLAN OF PROTECTION

You can have that knowledge, but it's when you believe it and speak it, that it begins to materialize in your life. That is why you don't have to give into fear. Fear is a real thing and the pandemic facing the world is absolutely real. But you don't have to give into the fear surrounding the pandemic.

CHAPTER 8
NOW WHAT?

The Lord never designed this life to be a drudgery. People ask me all the time where I get my energy and fire from. I can tell you - it's spending time with the Lord and the Holy Spirit. God is no respecter of persons and He will do it for anybody. It's so exciting to live for the Lord, walking this planet, as a believer, knowing who you are in God, and having the Holy Spirit come along side of you. He will work inside you to help you through problems, helping you through difficulties so that you can be a bold witness during this pandemic.

There's no better opportunity for us, as believers, to be the light. I like walking into stores and just smiling as people are wondering, "why is he so happy?" A few people have asked me what is behind my smile and it presents an incredible opportunity to share God's good news with them.

I've got an assignment for you. Read Psalm 91 every day and be specific to speak it over your life. You can choose to identify with the problems in your life or you can identify with the Word of God and bring your confession and your tongue in line with God's Word. As you begin to speak God's promise, all of that fear will be dispelled from your life. Fear runs when we begin to speak God's Word. Believe it or not, Jesus taught us to speak to mountains. There is life and death in the power of the tongue, so speak Psalm 91 over your life throughout the week.

We have to pray God's Word, believe it in our heart and then speak it. Stand against sickness and disease and curse it in the Name of Jesus. Curse it away from yourself and your family. You and I have authority over this horrid coronavirus - this plague that is trying to rampage our land.

OUR BATTLE CRY

This is our battle cry.

This is our confession.

This is our banner.

"No evil shall befall you, neither any plague come near your dwelling. For He shall give His angels charge over you to keep you in all your ways, a thousand will fall at your side and ten thousand at your right hand but it will not come near you, in Jesus Name. Amen."

HOW DO I KNOW?

How does a person really know where they go after death? The Bible is so clear on this. Heaven is real, Hell is real, eternity is real, and what you do with the person of Jesus Christ will determine your outcome. God loves you and He wants to give you the gift and the assurance of eternal life. The Bible tells us – whoever calls on the name of the Lord will be saved. Say this prayer right now: "Dear Lord, right now I repent of all my sin. Forgive me for breaking your laws and commands. I boldly confess Jesus Christ as my Savior and Lord. I choose to live for you all the days of my life. Thank you, Lord, for granting me the gift of eternal life. Amen."

"For God so loved the world that He gave His only begotten Son, that whoever believes in Him should not perish but have everlasting life." John 3:16

Romans 10, verses 9 and 13 says that "if you confess with your mouth the Lord Jesus and believe in your heart that God has raised Him from the dead, you will be saved. For whoever calls on the name of the Lord shall be saved."

Contact Information for Pastor John Galinetti

Pastor John Galinetti

8363 Embury Rd.

Grand Blanc, MI. 48439

Additional Information Available at:

Address: Mount Hope Church

8363 Embury Rd.

Grand Blanc, MI. 48439

Email: info@mhcgb.com

Phone: (810)695-0461

Fax: (810)695-7466

Website: www.mhcgb.com

Facebook: Facebook.com/mounthopegb

Instagram: @mounthopegb

LEARN HOW TO EXERCISE THE FAITH YOU ALREADY POSSESS IN JOHN GALINETTI'S FIRST BOOK, *PROGRESSIONS OF FAITH*

ORDER ON AMAZON.COM

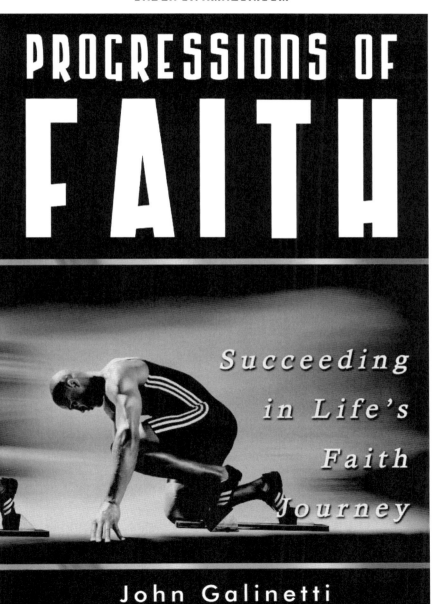

GET YOUR COPY OF *2% CHANCE TO LIVE* AT AMAZON.COM TODAY

In this practical and powerful guide, John Galinetti clearly explains:

- Where vision comes from (and where it doesn't)
- How to know you have vision (and if you don't)
- How to walk out your vision step by step
- How to guard your vision from attacks

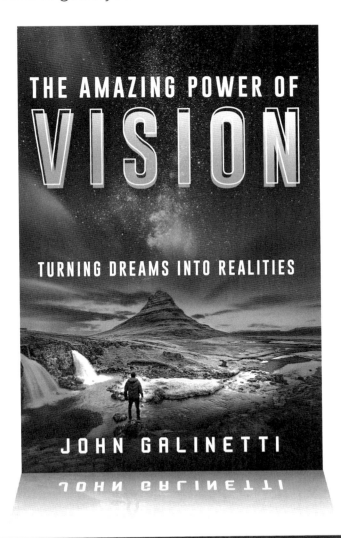

Available at Amazon.com

About John Galinetti

John Galinetti is the founding pastor of Mount Hope Church, a growing church in Grand Blanc, Michigan. He and his wife, Wendy, started the church in 1988. Relentlessly, Pastor John has dedicated himself to help people maximize their personal and spiritual potential for the cause of Christ.

Pastor John is heard daily on popular radio stations. His upbeat and motivating program called "The Pastor's Minute" reaches more than 60,000 commuters and offices who make it a regular part of their work day throughout Michigan. His passion and drive are evident as he continues to fervently preach the gospel in 18 nations including cultural centers, packed-out stadiums and sporting arenas.

Pastor John holds credentials with the Michigan District of the Assemblies of God and is a graduate of Global University and Rhema Bible Training College. He has authored four books, The Progressions of Faith, 2% Chance to Live, The Amazing Power of Vision, and Psalm 91 – God's Plan of Protection. He has also been featured on the 700 Club television program.

Pastor John is an outdoorsman and loves spending time with Wendy and their four children.